Tip Tip

T0337605

Written by Charlotte Raby

Illustrated by Afua Bediako

Collins

map

2

dad

map

dad

sit

. . .

pat

sit

pat

tip

nap

tip

nap

14

 Review: After reading

Use your assessment from hearing the children read to choose any GPCs and words that need additional practice.

Read 1: Decoding

- Use grapheme cards to make any words you need to practise. Model reading those words, using teacher-led blending.
- Look at the "I spy sounds" pages (14–15) together. Ask the children to point out as many things as they can in the picture that begin with the /d/ sound. (*dance, duck, ducklings, dress, dots, dog, den, dinosaur, doll, dummy, drink, dad*)
- Ask the children to follow as you read the whole book, demonstrating fluency and prosody.

Read 2: Vocabulary

- Look back through the book and discuss the pictures. Encourage the children to talk about details that stand out for them. Use a dialogic talk model to expand on their ideas and recast them in full sentences as naturally as possible.
- Work together to expand vocabulary by naming objects in the pictures that children do not know.
- On pages 10 and 11, ask: What word tells you that the baby is asleep? (*nap*)

Read 3: Comprehension

- Look at the picture on page 3. Encourage the children to describe a park that they have been to or would like to visit. Ask: What would you like to do at the park, and why?
- Read pages 6 and 7. Encourage the children to mime the actions for **sit** and **pat**. Ask: What is the boy sitting on? What else could you sit on at the park? (e.g. *a bench, a swing*) What else might you pat? (e.g *a dog, modelling clay*)
- Return to page 2 and talk about the map. Discuss what the map tells Mum and the children. (e.g. *it tells them what is at the park and how to get there*) Discuss any other maps the children have seen and what they are used for.